P9-DZM-482

J973.7
Lev

DISCARD

NAUVOO PUBLIC LIBRARY
NAUVOO, ILL.

DISCARD

NAUVOO PUBLIC LIBRARY
NAUVOO, ILL.

The First Book of

THE CIVIL WAR

The First Book of

The Civil War

By Dorothy Levenson

Franklin Watts
New York / London / 1977
Revised Edition

Cover design by Neil Stuart

Photographs courtesy of: Library of Congress: pp. ii, vi, 17, 24, 27 (bottom), 28, 32, 36, 44, 47, 53 (bottom); New York Historical Society, New York City: p. 5; Harper's Weekly: pp. 6, 50; The New York Public Library Picture Collection: pp. 18, 27 (top); The New York Public Library, Schomburg Center for Research in Black Culture: p. 39; U.S. Army: pp. 33; Culver Pictures, Inc.: p. 53 (top), National Archives: p. 57.

Library of Congress Cataloging in Publication Data

Levenson, Dorothy.
    The first book of the Civil War.

    (A First book)
    Bibliography: p.
    Includes index.
    SUMMARY: Discusses the history of the Civil War, the life of a soldier, slavery, taxes, and the position of women at the time.
    1. United States—History—Civil War, 1861–1865—Juvenile literature. [1. United States—History—Civil War, 1861–1865] I. Title.
E468.L54 1977   973.7   77–7153
ISBN 0-531-01291-3

Revised Edition
Copyright © 1968, 1977 by Franklin Watts, Inc.
All rights reserved
Printed in the United States of America
10 9 8 7

Contents

1

"A House Divided"

The great black leader, Frederick Douglass, was asked to speak at a July 4th celebration in 1852. Douglass wondered why:

". . . Why am I called upon to speak here today? What have I, or those I represent, to do with your national independence? What to the American slave is your Fourth of July? To him, your celebration is a sham; your boasted liberty, an unholy license. . . . There is not a nation on the earth guilty of practices more shocking and bloody, than are the people of these United States, at this very hour."

Douglass had been born a slave. He had escaped to freedom, but there were still 3 million black slaves in the United States. These men, women, and children had no right to "life, liberty and the pursuit of happiness."

☆ THE SLAVES

Slaves had no rights. Masters had the right to whip their slaves. In most Southern states, the law said that no one could teach a slave to read or write. Slave children could be taken from their parents and sold to a faraway plantation. If slaves tried to escape, they were chased by dogs and by men with guns.

Early settlers in this country brought black slaves with them. Thousands of Africans were kidnapped and brought to America, where they could be sold like any other possession. Black slaves had to work, without pay, for the person who bought them. They belonged to the farmer just like horses or cattle. They were expected to breed like horses or cattle to produce more slaves for the master and mistress.

The men who wrote the Declaration of Independence accepted slavery as a part of life in the United States. By 1850 the Northern states had abolished slavery. The 3 million black slaves were in the South. When Frederick Douglass spoke, the nation was deeply divided.

Most farms in the North were small enough to be worked by the farmer and his family. Factory owners in the North found that men and women worked harder for wages than they did if they were slaves.

The warm lands of the South were good for growing cotton, tobacco, and sugar. All these crops needed many people to grow and harvest them. The factories of old England and New England paid high prices for cotton. More and more land was found that was good for growing cotton: the rich black soil of Alabama, Mississippi, and Louisiana, the wide plains of Texas.

Planters hurried west from Virginia, taking their slaves with them to build new plantations in the wilderness. More and more slaves were brought from Africa. The old states of the South—Virginia and the Carolinas—found a new crop. Farmers raised black children to sell, in the same way other farmers raised hogs and sheep. The Afro-American slave became a valuable commodity.

Each plantation became almost a world in itself, with the great house where the family lived and the little cabins where the slaves lived. All the crops were "cash crops," grown not to be used by the farmer but to be sold for money. The cotton and tobacco and sugar were sent to the factories and markets of the North and of Europe. The South was dependent on trade with the North and with other nations. The South sold farm crops and bought from the Northern states and from other countries the things she did not produce herself. The South bought cloth and dishes, guns and glassware, machines and railroad cars. Almost anything made in a factory had to be brought into the South from some other place.

There were also small farms in the South. On some, farmers made a good living. In the western parts of Virginia and Kentucky and Tennessee were poor, small hill farms. The soil was thin. Farmers lived as much by hunting as by farming.

There were few cities in the South and almost no factories. If a man or woman could not make a living on a farm, there were few other ways to live.

Southerners feared that the North was growing stronger all the time. By 1860 the North had 22 million people. The South had 9 million and more than a third of these were slaves. Across the North stretched 22,000 miles of railroad. The South had 9,000. Eighty percent of the goods and services produced in the whole country were produced in the North. The North had 105 million acres of farmland. The South had only 57 million.

The Northern states were big, bustling, and growing. Settlements were scattered all the way from the Atlantic to the Pacific.

In the East there were rich farms with strong, well-built barns to protect the farm animals in the fierce winters. In the north woods there were clearings where log cabins were surrounded by the patches of grain and vegetables that the farmers raised in summer. In winter the farmers turned to trapping. The wide plains of the Middle West were dotted with fields of corn. In California, gold was discovered. Thousands of people set out for the West Coast—some overland, some by ship around Cape Horn. The gold discovered in the "Goldrush" helped pay the bills for the Civil War.

There were big cities in the North. Chicago was growing, and New York had almost a million people. Factories were built all through New England. Their machinery was kept turning by the waterpower of the many small rivers that tumbled down the hills. The cities and factory towns were dirty. The streets were muddy. Wages were low, and men, women, and

Slaves were bought and sold like cattle. Regular sales were held in big cities. Advertisements pointed out the good qualities of the slaves being sold. Words like "Mulatto" (for a man) and "Mulatress" (for a woman) indicated that they were part-white.

HEWLETT & BRIGHT.

SALE OF

VALUABLE SLAVES,

(On account of departure)

The Owner of the following named and valuable Slaves, being on the eve of departure for Europe, will cause the same to be offered for sale, at the NEW EXCHANGE, corner of St. Louis and Chartres streets, on *Saturday,* May 16, at Twelve o'Clock, *viz.*

1. **SARAH,** a mulatress, aged 45 years, a good cook and accustomed to house work in general, is an excellent and faithful nurse for sick persons, and in every respect a first rate character.

2. **DENNIS,** her son, a mulatto, aged 24 years, a first rate cook and steward for a vessel, having been in that capacity for many years on board one of the Mobile packets; is strictly honest, temperate, and a first rate subject.

3. **CHOLE,** a mulatress, aged 36 years, she is, without execption, one of the most competent servants in the country, a first rate washer and ironer, does up lace, a good cook, and for a bachelor who wishes a house-keeper she would be invaluable; she is also a good ladies' maid, having travelled to the North in that capacity.

4. **FANNY,** her daughter, a mulatress, aged 16 years, speaks French and English, is a superior hair-dresser, (pupil of Guilliac,) a good seamstress and ladies' maid, is smart, intelligent, and a first rate character.

5. **DANDRIDGE,** a mulatoo, aged 26 years, a first rate dining-room servant, a good painter and rough carpenter, and has but few equals for honesty and sobriety.

6. **NANCY,** his wife, aged about 24 years, a confidential house servant, good seamstress, mantuamaker and tailoress, a good cook, washer and ironer, etc.

7. **MARY ANN,** her child, a creole, aged 7 years, speaks French and English, is smart, active and intelligent.

8. **FANNY or FRANCES,** a mulatress, aged 22 years, is a first rate washer and ironer, good cook and house servant, and has an excellent character.

9. **EMMA,** an orphan, aged 10 or 11 years, speaks French and English, has been in the country 7 years, has been accustomed to waiting on table, sewing etc.; is intelligent and active.

10. **FRANK,** a mulatto, aged about 32 years speaks French and English, is a first rate hostler and coachman, understands perfectly well the management of horses, and is, in every respect, a first rate character, with the exception that he will occasionally drink, though not an habitual drunkard.

☞ All the above named Slaves are acclimated and excellent subjects; they were purchased by their present vendor many years ago, and will, therefore, be severally warranted against all vices and maladies prescribed by law, save and except FRANK, who is fully guaranteed in every other respect but the one above mentioned.

Women were allowed to travel with
the army to wash the men's clothes.
They were paid by each soldier.

children worked long hard hours. But there was opportunity. Farm boys and girls came to the cities and the factory towns to make money. Immigrants from Europe arrived on every boat.

The North was changing from a land of farms to one where industry was important. The North was changing more quickly than the South. It would be the factories of the North that won the Civil War.

☆ WOMEN

Most people in the North and South agreed about one thing—the place of women. Women could not vote. A woman could not be elected as president or as a member of Congress. Women could not be elected to office in any town or city or state. Most colleges would not admit women. There were not many ways in which a woman could earn a living. She could be a factory hand or a schoolteacher or a servant. She could work in a store or as a waitress. If a married woman went out to work, the money she earned belonged to her husband.

Women were expected to marry early and have large families of ten or twelve children.

Men felt that women were weak. They said that women must stay at home and be protected by men. But women who stayed at home worked hard. Housework with no machines to help was much harder work than it is today. There were no washing machines or dishwashers or vacuum cleaners. The family clothes and sheets and blankets had to be washed by hand and hung out to dry. Rugs were taken up, hung over the clothesline outside, and beaten to get rid of dust. Taking care of so many children was hard work. All the diapers for all those babies had to be washed by hand.

Women who went out to work were badly paid. In 1855 Lucy Stone, who wanted to change the way women were treated, said:

"Women working in tailor shops are paid one-third as much as men . . . in Philadelphia . . . women make fine shirts for twelve and a half cents apiece; . . . no women can make more than nine a week, and the sum thus earned, after deducting rent, fuel, etc., leaves her just three and a half cents a day for bread. . . . Female teachers in New York are paid fifty dollars a year, and for every such situation there are five hundred applications."

Men were almost always paid more than women. In 1850 a plumber working in Massachusetts would have made $600 a year.

Sojourner Truth, a black woman, sneered at the men who talked about women as the "weaker sex":

"That man over there says that women need to be helped into carriages, and lifted over ditches, and to have the best place everywhere. Nobody ever helps me into carriages, or over mud puddles, or gives me any best place! And ain't I a woman? Look at me! Look at my arm! I have ploughed and planted, and gathered into barns, and no man could head me! And ain't I a woman? I could work as much and eat as much as a man—when I could get it—and bear the lash as well! And ain't I a woman? I have borne thirteen children, and seen most all sold off to slavery, and when I cried out with my mother's grief, none but Jesus heard me! And ain't I a woman?"

Some women asked to be equal. They held meetings. They petitioned Congress. Most men did not listen. Many women did not listen either. They were content with the way they lived. But the women's movement became strong and worked closely with the antislavery movement.

2

Conflict and

Compromise

The argument about whether or not there should be slaves in the United States went on for a long time. People talked and fought and killed each other over it for many years before the Civil War. They argued in the courts and in Congress, in churches and newspapers. Sometimes their weapons were words—and sometimes guns.

There were about half a million free black people in the United States. Some of these, like Sojourner Truth and Frederick Douglass, were escaped slaves. Truth and Douglass spent their lives talking to white people, trying to persuade them to fight for the freedom of all black people.

Harriet Tubman was also an escaped slave. She spent her life going back down South to help other slaves escape. Blacks and sympathetic whites set up the "Underground Railroad." This was not really a railroad but a secret organization formed by people all over the country who wanted to help slaves escape to the Northern states or to Canada. Since slaves were legally the possessions of their masters, the organization was kept secret because what they were doing was against the law. Slaves were helped to run away. They were smuggled from house to house, usually traveling at night, often in disguise, sometimes hidden under a load of hay in a farmer's wagon, until they reached a place where they could live free.

Some slaves, like Nat Turner, rose in rebellion. They tried to fight their way out of slavery. None of these uprisings was successful.

In the North some free blacks and whites worked together. They wrote books and newspapers and spoke at meetings saying that all people should be free. They were called ABOLITION-ISTS because they wanted to abolish slavery. In the years before the Civil War, the most popular book in the country was *Uncle Tom's Cabin,* written by a white woman, Harriet Beecher Stowe. The book described the slave system as being so horrible that thousands of people were convinced that slavery had to end.

Even free blacks had many problems. Most Northerners did not like slavery—but that did not mean they could accept black people as equals. In many Northern towns, blacks had to live in the poorest part of town. Their children had to go to separate schools from white children. Blacks found it hard to get jobs. Illinois would not allow black people to live in that state.

☆ THE MISSOURI COMPROMISE

People in the North did not want slavery to spread. There were millions of acres of land open for settlement. Northerners wanted free farmers to settle there, not plantation owners and their slaves.

People from both North and South moved westward all

the time, farming new land. When enough people had gathered in a new area, they asked to become a state. Most of the people who settled in Missouri were slaveowners. When the people of Missouri asked to come into the Union as a state, people in the free states were afraid. Too many slaveholders in Congress meant too many votes against the free states. It was decided in 1820 that Missouri could come in as a slave state, if Maine could come in as a free state. That was the way it remained for several years. When a slave state was admitted, so was a free one. The MISSOURI COMPROMISE said that slavery was prohibited in any new state north of the southern boundary of Pennsylvania, or 36° 30′ north latitude.

As the years went by, people began to feel more and more strongly about slavery. More and more people in the North wanted to do away with slavery completely. More and more people in the South felt that Northerners were interfering with their way of life—helping their slaves escape, stirring up discontent.

From 1850 to 1860 it seemed that almost everyone in the country was arguing about slavery all the time. In 1850 Congress worked out another compromise with measures that pleased almost nobody. It said, among other things, that California was to come in as a free state. Utah and New Mexico could come in as they chose, either slave or free. Slaves could no longer be bought and sold in the District of Columbia, but the laws about runaway slaves were made much more strict.

Congress went on arguing. In Kansas settlers argued and then began shooting. Kansas was on the border between North and South, and settlers came there from both parts of the country. In 1854 Congress repealed the Missouri Compromise. The people who lived in a new state were now to decide for themselves whether their state was to be slave or free. Some settlers in Kansas wanted slaves. Some did not. They tried to settle the issue by killing each other.

☆ THE SUPREME COURT AND SLAVERY

In 1857 the Supreme Court joined the argument. Dred Scott was a slave who lived in Missouri. His master took him on a trip to Illinois, which was a free state, and then into Wisconsin, a free territory. Dred Scott felt that since he had lived in a free state and a free territory he should be free. He went to court and asked the judge to say that he was free. The Supreme Court decided that because Dred Scott was black he could not be a citizen of the United States and therefore could not bring suit in a Federal court. The Court also said that Congress had no right to prohibit slavery. Slaves and abolitionists knew that they could not look to the Court for help.

The Court's decision did not change people's minds. The arguments went on. Abraham Lincoln first became famous all over the country when, in 1858, he debated the issue of slavery with Stephen A. Douglas who was running against him for the position of senator from Illinois. People came long distances on horseback and on foot to hear the two candidates speak. Newspapers across the nation carried stories about the debates.

☆ THE CANDIDATES DEBATE

Lincoln and Douglas disagreed about whether slavery should be allowed in the territories of the United States. At that time, there were still large parts of the country where there were not enough settlers to create a state government. Those areas were called territories and were ruled directly from Washington. Lincoln said that there should be no slaves in the territories. Douglas said: "If each state will only agree to mind its own business, and let its neighbors alone, . . . this republic can exist forever divided into free and slave states, as our fathers made it and the people of each state have decided."

Lincoln did not agree with this either. He declared: "A house divided against itself cannot stand. I believe this government cannot endure, permanently half slave and half free."

Douglas won the Senate seat, but people remembered the tall lawyer from Illinois when he ran for president two years later.

The men who thought guns were better than words went on fighting. John Brown, one of the men who had fought against slavery in Kansas, tried to lead a slave rebellion in Virginia. Federal troops defeated him and his small band of friends, both black and white. John Brown was hanged, but when the Civil War broke out, men from the North marched into battle singing:

John Brown's body lies a-mouldering in the grave,
But his soul goes marching on.

Only a few men fought beside John Brown at Harper's Ferry, but he frightened Southerners. They began to believe that the North would do anything to abolish slavery.

In 1860, when Abraham Lincoln ran for president, most people believed that when they voted they were voting for or against slavery. But there were other issues, too.

Lincoln ran as a candidate for the Republican Party. At that time, the Republican Party stood for high tariffs. (A tariff is a tax paid on goods coming into a country from foreign lands.) The South opposed the tariffs and had argued against them for a long time. Indeed, more than thirty years before, South Carolina threatened to leave the Union over this very issue. The farmers of the South, who wanted to sell their cotton to other counties and buy manufactured things they needed as cheaply as they could, were strongly against tariffs. But the factory owners of the North wanted to be able to sell their own cloth and iron and the other things they made in the United States. They wanted to keep out foreign goods. The best way to do this was by raising tariffs in order to make foreign goods more expensive.

As the North and South argued about slavery, they also argued about tariffs.

When Abraham Lincoln was elected president in 1860, most people in the South believed that he would raise tariffs and free the slaves.

3

War!

On March 4, 1861, Abraham Lincoln became president. The people of Washington, D.C. waited, tense and anxious as soldiers lined Pennsylvania Avenue. With guns at the ready, they watched for anyone who might try to shoot the new leader of the nation.

The whole country expected trouble. Lincoln was being sworn in as President of the United States, but the states were no longer united. A few months before, there had been thirty-four states in the Union. Since that time, seven states—South Carolina, Mississippi, Florida, Alabama, Georgia, Louisiana, and Texas—had said that they no longer wanted to be part of the United States.

Men from those seven states met in Montgomery, Alabama, in February to form a new nation, the Confederate States of America. Jefferson Davis was their president.

Now there were two presidents—one in Washington and one in Montgomery. There were two nations—the UNION and the CONFEDERACY—and two armies ready to fight.

Abraham Lincoln was no abolitionist. He did not like slavery. He did not want slavery to spread into new parts of the country, but he was not ready to go to war to bring about the end of slavery. In the speech he made when he became president, Lincoln said that slavery was legal in the South and he would not interfere. But he said that no state could lawfully leave the Union and that he had taken an oath to "preserve, protect and defend" the government of the United States.

Abraham Lincoln believed in the United States of America. He believed that this was one nation. For that he would fight. For that he would lead his people through four years of warfare so that they should remain "one nation indivisible."

The Civil War was only the second war to be photographed. (The first was the Crimean War in 1854.) To take a picture, the photographer coated a sheet of glass with chemicals. This "plate" had to be used within five minutes of the time it was coated. The subject had to stand still for at least a minute and a half. Once the photograph was taken, it had to be developed within five minutes. Photographers trundled along with the army in a wagon loaded with supplies. The wagon served as a portable darkroom.

☆ THE WAR BEGINS

On an island in the harbor of Charleston, South Carolina, stood Fort Sumter. Federal troops held the fort. The rations were running low. The Confederate government stopped food supplies from going into the fort and demanded that the soldiers surrender.

Lincoln had to decide what to do. Should he withdraw the troops from Confederate territory, or should he send them supplies?

The President decided that the power of the United States government must be upheld. He could not surrender a Federal fort without a fight. He sent food to the soldiers in Fort Sumter. On April 12, 1861, Confederate troops fired on the fort. The Civil War had begun.

Virginia, Arkansas, Tennessee, and North Carolina joined the Confederacy. No one was sure what the states on the border between the North and South—Missouri, Kentucky, Delaware, and Maryland—would do. In the end, they remained with the Union. Part of Virginia joined the North and became the new state of West Virginia.

The South quickly took Fort Sumter. The next important battle took place near Washington.

Abraham Lincoln (in the stovepipe hat) visiting an army camp. Because so many battles were fought close to Washington, D.C., Lincoln often visited the men and the officers.

☆ BATTLE AT BULL RUN

Anyone who looked down on the Virginia countryside on July 21, 1861, would have seen one of the strangest sights ever seen in any war. There was the Union Army, the men hot and thirsty as they straggled along the dusty roads toward Manassas Junction on Bull Run Creek, thirty-five miles south of the capital.

There were not only soldiers on the road. Coming along behind the army was a gay and elegant procession of coaches and riders on horseback. People were setting out from Washington to have a Sunday picnic and to see a battle at the same time. There were senators and congressmen and pretty girls with parasols. All had come to see the two armies—North and South—meet for the first time.

Few people in the United States, or in the Confederate States, had ever seen a battle. They thought of war as a kind of game. They forgot that men would be hurt and killed. The Washington sightseers expected the war to end quickly, and they wanted to see some of the action before it was all over.

General William T. Sherman knew that it would not be so easy. "This war will take four years and an army of two million men before the rebellion can be crushed," he said. Few people believed him.

So here came the crowds, following the army through the green Virginia countryside, ready for a picnic with champagne and cold chicken.

The South was not much better prepared. Girls threw flowers at the Confederate soldiers marching to Manassas. Women set up tables along the roadside to serve lemonade to the troops.

Suddenly the armies met and the picnic was over. Guns roared. Men dropped, dead or wounded.

At first the Union troops seemed to be winning, but Southern reinforcements arrived. The troops on both sides were new and inexperienced. Most of them had never been in battle before. At the first setback, the Yankees panicked. Back along the road to Washington they ran, throwing away rifles, blankets, haversacks, and ammunition.

When all the happy picnickers from Washington saw what was happening, they ran too. The road to Washington became a screaming mass of people and horses.

Ambulances and army wagons were mixed up with the sightseers and coaches and buggies. Girls dropped their parasols and ran. Politicians scooted down the dusty road.

All through Sunday and Monday the army straggled back into Washington. The city was terrified. Leaderless soldiers wandered the streets. No one knew what to do. If the Southern army had attacked right then, they would have taken Washington. But the South was not ready for war either. There was celebration around Confederate campfires, but no army marched on Washington.

Both sides waited, knowing that time was needed to raise and train more troops.

☆ THE GENERALS

The Southerners moved their capital to Richmond, Virginia, only 100 miles from Washington. Northern newspapers blazed the words, "On to Richmond!" across their front pages, but the Union Army took four years to cover those 100 miles. Richmond did not fall until the end of the war.

The greatest asset of the Confederacy was General Robert E. Lee, who had been called the "greatest soldier in the United States" before the war. After the fall of Fort Sumter, Lincoln asked Lee to command the Union Army. He refused and rode south to fight for his own state of Virginia.

Lincoln had trouble finding a soldier as good as Lee. After the chaos at Bull Run, Lincoln asked General George B. McClellan to organize the army. McClellan drilled the army. He made sure that the uniforms were clean and the brass polished. He trained the men to march and parade, but then McClellan did not know what to do with his beautiful army. Finally, Lincoln had to order McClellan to attack.

General McClellan approached Richmond cautiously. He hesitated and dawdled. He believed every report that said Lee's army was larger than his. After a couple of battles that did not decide anything, he turned around and came back to Washington.

Lincoln dismissed McClellan and replaced him with General John Pope. Then Lee almost broke through to the North. Lincoln called back McClellan. In September McClellan stopped Lee at Sharpsburg, Maryland, near Antietam Creek. There the armies fought the bloodiest battle of the war until that time. But McClellan slowed down again. He did not follow through with an attack. Lincoln dismissed McClellan again. He appointed General Ambrose E. Burnside, who was a man with magnificent whiskers but not much ability.

For three years the Army of Northern Virginia, under General Lee, was able to keep the Union Army and its nervous generals marching up and down through Virginia, Maryland, and Pennsylvania. The South could not win this war—but could defend itself very well.

[22]

4

The Armies

In 1861 neither North nor South had an army large enough to fight a war effectively. The Confederacy was a new nation starting out with none of the organization necessary to run a country or fight a war. The South busily set about creating an army and a navy.

The Federal government had a small army. President Lincoln asked for 75,000 men to join the army for three months. Like most other people, the President did not expect a long war.

Three months! That was hardly enough time to teach a recruit to be a soldier. Many of these volunteers had never ridden a horse, or handled a gun, or even walked very far. These armies had to walk—and walk—and walk. There were few railroads, no automobiles. In good weather, when roads were dry, soldiers marched as much as thirty miles a day.

Most roads were not paved. In summer, a few thousand men walking along a dirt road churned up a cloud of dust.

NAUVOO PUBLIC LIBRARY
NAUVOO, ILL.

Army cooks and kitchens were rough-and-ready. Worse yet, there was no understanding of nutrition. Soldiers suffered from scurvy and other diseases because of the bad food.

Marching was hot, thirsty work. Soldiers learned to throw away anything they did not really need. Civilians could tell if new or old soldiers had passed by. New soldiers littered the roadside with blankets and equipment thrown away as they tired. Old soldiers did not throw things away. They were tougher and their extras had all been thrown away long before.

Horses pulled what the men could not carry. Horses were used in the Civil War for men to ride into battle, but many more of them were used to haul loads.

All the supplies, food for the horses and the men, and all the other things they needed rolled along in heavy wagons. Ambulances were pulled by horses. Each big gun needed a crew of five to fire it. An artillery company was made up of about 150 men, 80 horses, and 6 guns.

An army on the move was an impressive sight; men marching in columns, flags flying, horses hauling the rumbling wagons. All those men and horses and wagons moved slowly and clumsily. While they were moving through enemy territory, snipers or cavalry raiders picked men off from the outer ranks.

Moving an army in rainy weather was always a nightmare and often impossible. The rains quickly turned the dusty roads to mud, and feet and hooves churned the mud to a heavy bog. Big guns and wagons stuck fast. Old soldiers made jokes about mud so deep that they could only see the horses' ears.

Armies tried to avoid fighting in winter when snow and rain bogged down the wagon trains. Many more Civil War battles took place in fine summer weather than in winter. That was one of the ways in which war had not changed. Just as George Washington and his men spent the winter in camp at Valley Forge, so Civil War soldiers spent most of their winters in camp.

War was a summertime business for thousands of years. Not until roads had been paved and armies moved by truck would wars be fought during all times of the year.

Soldiers marched along a road in a long narrow column. Once the battlefield was reached, the shape of the column changed. Then the men lined up to face the enemy. During the battle, hundreds of men, moving together, obeyed complicated orders. With smoke and shot and shell whirling around, whole armies followed the orders shouted by their officers.

Long hours of training on a drill field were necessary before troops were ready to maneuver on a battlefield. Soldiers never liked drilling. A man joined up eager to get into a fight. He wanted to take a few shots at the enemy, not spend hours marching backwards and forwards on a dusty field. In the early days of the war, there were not enough trained officers, and recruits were often drilled by men who did not know any more than they did.

Before the war was over, the Union Army had grown to over a million men. The Confederacy probably never had more than half that number.

☆ WEAPONS AND UNIFORMS

Most Civil War soldiers carried a rifled musket. Old-fashioned smooth-bore muskets were not very accurate. Rifled muskets had grooves inside the barrel that guided the bullet much more accurately. But even these new weapons could not be fired very fast. Before a soldier could fire his musket, he had to bite open a paper cartridge, pour powder down the musket barrel, push the bullet in with a ramrod, cock the hammer,

Above: the chief weapon carried by soldiers in the Civil War was a rifled musket. "Rifling"—the grooves inside the barrel—made this weapon much more accurate than the old muskets. A bayonet was attached to the front for soldiers to use in close fighting. Below: the swab under the barrel of this large gun was for cleaning the barrel between shots. Most Civil War guns were "smooth bore," that is, their barrels were not rifled, and they were not very accurate. Sometimes, they were used to fire large round "Cannon balls." Other times, they fired canister—a tin can full of lead slugs. The can broke to pieces in the air, and the lead pieces flew all over, wounding many men.

Many Civil War battles were fought by lines of
men charging with rifles and fixed bayonets across
open fields against other lines of men armed in
the same way. Officers led their men in the charge.
Each regiment carried its own flag or "colors."

and set the percussion cap. New soldiers spent weeks trying to learn to do this quickly, but even the rifle fire from experienced soldiers was slow.

Heavy guns were also loaded by pouring in the powder and then the charge. Between shots the barrel was swabbed out. If a spark remained from the previous shot, the powder exploded as it was poured in. The guns were almost as dangerous to the men firing them as to the enemy. Most heavy guns were smooth bores and not very accurate, but when fired against a mass of advancing infantry, they were deadly.

If the defending troops had time to dig trenches to protect themselves, they could hold off an attack indefinitely. The men in both armies began to realize this long before the generals did. Officers noticed that whenever troops halted they began to dig trenches before any orders had been given.

Many Civil War battles were fought in the old style—lines of men charging against each other. Some of the worst killing of the war, and the most useless, took place when troops were sent to charge uphill against an enemy protected by trenches or barricades.

Generals led these charges. (The Civil War was oversupplied with generals. The Union Army had 2,537). Generals often rode on horseback, while their men were on foot. A general on a horse made a fine target for an enemy sharpshooter. The Civil War is full of tragic stories of brave generals killed in battle. Color bearers also made fine targets. They carried the regimental flags into battle, to lead the way for other soldiers. The proudest boast a regiment could make was that its flag had never touched the ground. A man always rushed forward to catch the flag if the bearer was shot.

"The Blue and the Gray" has become the name for the soldiers of the Civil War, as if all Northern troops wore blue uniforms and all Southern troops wore gray. That was not always true.

The official uniform of the Northern armies was blue, but many regiments chose their own uniforms. A famous New York company of volunteers wore baggy red pants and short red jackets. The Iron Brigade of Michigan wore wide-brimmed black hats, each with a feather curling up the side. The United States Sharpshooters wore dark green uniforms, leather leggings, and feathers in their hats.

Uniforms were scarce for Southern soldiers. Before the war, the South sent almost all its cotton to Europe or the Northern states to be made into cloth. There were no factories in the South to make uniforms. Women in the South learned from their grandmothers or from their poorer neighbors how to weave homespun cloth. They made dye for the cloth from butternuts. Soon the most common color worn by Confederate soldiers was not gray but the warm brown of butternuts.

The Confederate Army was not as well supplied as the Yankees. The North had the industrial resources to turn out the weapons of war. The mines of the North produced the iron that was molded into cannons in the great foundries. There was only one place in the South that could make cannons. There was only one small mill to make gunpowder for the whole Confederate Army.

☆ CAMPS AND CASUALTIES

Camp life was neither comfortable nor healthy on either side. For every man in the Confederate Army who died in battle, three died from disease. The death rate was almost as high in the Union Army. Men died of scurvy because they did not get fresh fruit or vegetables to eat. Army rations were usually hardtack (a kind of hard cracker), coffee, and salt pork. Typhoid, dysentery, malaria, pneumonia, and even measles swept through the camps.

Much of the disease was caused by dirt. In most camps there was no way to keep clean. Most of the time the men lived in filth. Everyone itched from lice. The drinking water was often dirty.

The men had little shelter from cold or heat. Each Union soldier was given a piece of canvas about five feet by five feet. That was his tent. To use it he needed another soldier with a piece of canvas. The two men put up two forked sticks about six feet apart. They placed another stick over the forked sticks, buttoned their canvases together along the middle, and stretched the joined piece across the sticks. The result was a rough kind of tent. Unless the two soldiers were very short, their feet stuck out of the tent when they lay down to sleep. Rain came in the open ends.

Sometimes larger tents were used. Twelve men slept in these in a circle—their feet together in the middle and their heads against the walls of the tent.

When the men settled in winter camp, they built shelters for themselves. Four men built a hut together. Logs were used for the walls, and the tent halves were used for a roof. Bunks were built to fit two men in each. They helped keep each other warm.

Casualties were very high in the Civil War. Accurate figures are hard to collect, especially for the South, but it has been estimated that as many Americans died in the Civil War

Thousands of Union soldiers died in Andersonville Prison in Georgia. There were no real buildings. There were no toilets. There was no water supply, except a small stream that ran over the bare ground. The earth became a filthy quagmire, full of germs. Every small scratch that a man had became infected. Right: The Confederate Congress designed several flags. The battle flag— shown here—was a red square with a blue cross from corner to corner with a white star for each state. There were many others: state flags, regiment flags, and others designed by the Confederate Congress.

as in all the other United States wars combined until 1960. Men died from disease. They died from infected wounds. They died in prison. Only a small percentage was actually killed in battle.

A man wounded in battle was first taken to a crude field hospital. Aware of the great danger of infection, doctors cut off injured arms and legs. But while they knew of the danger of infection, they did not understand the cause. They operated with dirty hands and dirty instruments. Field hospitals were terrifying places to visit. Lined up outside, standing if they could or lying on the ground, were the wounded. As they waited for treatment, they could hear the screams of the men being operated on. Anesthetics existed, but they were in short supply, especially in the South. Often an operation was performed with nothing to deaden the pain for the patient except a shot of whiskey.

Soldiers who were captured were taken to a prison camp. Thousands of prisoners on both sides died because of bad food and filthy conditions in the camps. Andersonville Prison in Georgia was one of the worst. The prison was a bare piece of ground surrounded by a high fence. As many as 32,000 Union prisoners were packed in at one time with scarcely enough room to walk around in. A small stream provided the only water for drinking or washing. There were no toilets. The men had no shelter and little food. The prison became so dirty that the smallest scratch became infected. In one six-month period, 13,000 men died.

The Union sent many of its prisoners as far north as possible to make escape more difficult. They were kept in unheated barracks in the severe northern winters. Thousands died there of pneumonia.

5

The Black Struggle

When the Civil War began, most white people in the North were not fighting a war to end slavery. They were fighting to save the Union—to keep all the states of the United States together as one nation. Most of them agreed with Abraham Lincoln when he wrote:

"If I could save the Union without freeing any slave, I would do it; if I could save it by freeing all the slaves, I would do it; and if I could save it by freeing some and leaving others alone, I would also do that. What I do about slavery and the colored race, I do because I believe it helps to save the Union. . . ."

That was not the way black people saw the war. They wanted to defeat the South and end slavery forever. They felt that this was their fight, and they wanted to be part of it.

In the North free blacks wanted to join the army, but they found that they were not wanted. Many white people in the

*Black soldiers faced prejudice all the time. Almost none of
them became officers. They were put in segregated units
commanded by white officers. These men were part of the
107th United States Colored Infantry. Black people have been
called by many different names in the United States. Some of
the names have been "negro," "colored," and "Afro-American."*

North—both civilians and soldiers—were against allowing black soldiers in the army. They did allow blacks as laborers, cooks, teamsters, and servants to wait on the white soldiers. However, blacks were not allowed to carry guns. A black regiment was formed, but soon disbanded and the men were told to go home.

When the army found that there were not enough white men enlisting, black men were finally allowed to join the Union Army. They enlisted enthusiastically. One hundred and eighty-six thousand blacks served in the Union Army. Others joined the navy.

Black men were still not treated as equals. They were almost never allowed to become officers. They were paid less than white soldiers.

But black men were fighting for a cause in which they believed. They were fighting to free black slaves. The black regiments fought bravely under their white officers. Twenty-two black men won the Congressional Medal of Honor.

Black soldiers stood up proudly against prejudice. One black regiment insisted on serving for a whole year without pay rather than accept less pay than white soldiers were given.

☆ FREEDOM WHEN?

If white people were confused about how to treat free blacks, they were just as confused about what to do with slaves. In 1861, General John Charles Frémont said that the slaves who belonged to rebellious planters in Missouri should be free. (Missouri was a border state fighting on the side of the North.) President Lincoln said they must remain slaves. Lincoln felt that to win the war he needed the support of all white people in the North and in the border states between the North and South.

He did not want to anger those who believed in slavery.

But, of course, that was not the way the slaves saw the war. From the beginning, they thought of the war as a war for freedom—their freedom.

The news of the war spread through the slave quarters of the South. Most slaves could not read or write. They could not buy newspapers with war news or write to their friends. But they had long years of practice at passing news among themselves and keeping secrets from their masters. War news was whispered to friends. A sign language developed. The way a slave walked or wore a hat gave friends a piece of information. Both armies knew that a slave grapevine carried word of army defeats and victories from Virginia to Texas.

Some slaves had no choice. They were forced to help the Confederate Army. When young plantation owners went off to war, they often took a slave along with them as a servant. Slaves were used throughout the war as laborers to dig trenches, build fortifications, and repair roads for Southern armies. Some slaves felt a sense of loyalty to the white families with whom they lived and they tried to help as the war raged around the plantations of the South.

Most slaves, however, tried to help "Mr. Lincoln's army" when they could. Many men who had run away from slavery before the war came back as scouts for the Northern armies because they knew the country so well. Whenever a Northerner escaped from Southern prison, he tried to find a black field hand to feed him, help him, and guide him to the North again.

All over the South, as soon as a Northern army appeared, slaves ran away to join it or ask for protection. Northern generals did not know what to do with these escaping slaves. Some generals tried to solve the problem by sending the slaves back

Major Martin R. Delany was appointed by President Lincoln as the first black field officer in the United States Army. Delany, whom Lincoln called "this most extraordinary and intelligent black man," graduated from Harvard medical school and was an explorer, writer, and fighter for black rights before the Civil War. Long before the war, he called on black people to do "some fearless, bold, and adventurous deeds of daring."

to their masters. Some built special camps for the black men, women, and children. There were not enough supplies to feed and clothe everybody.

General Ben Butler helped to solve the question. He was from Massachusetts, a state that had always had many abolitionists. Ben Butler realized that Congress was not yet ready to free the slaves. So, he agreed that these black people still belonged to their masters. But, said Ben Butler, in wartime an invading army usually could confiscate the property of the enemy. He confiscated the slaves he met. He said they were "contraband of war" and set them to work for his army, helping to defeat their masters. Congress understood and forbade any Union officer to return slaves to their masters.

Ben Butler went further. He found that free black men in New Orleans, Louisiana were anxious to fight for the Union. They had already formed a regiment and when Butler asked what they wanted to do, their leader replied: ". . . we come of a fighting race. We are willing to fight . . . the only cowardly blood we have got in our veins is the white blood."

The general organized these Southerners into the first officially recognized black regiment in the Union Army. They were called the First Louisiana Native Guards.

Congress and the President agreed with the runaway slaves and Ben Butler. During 1862 all the slaves in the territories were declared free. Then, all runaway slaves were declared free. At last, on New Year's Day, 1863, Lincoln issued the EMANCIPATION PROCLAMATION, which said that all slaves in the states in rebellion against the United States, "shall be, then, thenceforward and forever free."

There was wild celebration among both black people and their white friends, and, yet, the Emancipation Proclamation did not actually free many slaves. There were still slaves in the border states—Kentucky, Missouri, Delaware, and Maryland—and in areas of the South controlled by the Union government. Lincoln felt that he had to move carefully. Slavery was not made illegal in the whole country until two years later when Congress approved the Thirteenth Amendment to the Constitution.

The more slavery became an issue in the war, the more many white people in the North resented the fact. They blamed black people for the war. As the fighting dragged on, fewer men volunteered for the army. In the spring of 1863, almost two years after the war started, Congress passed the first conscription law. Men were to be drafted into the army whether they wanted to go or not.

The law was especially hard on poor people. If a man's name was called, he could be excused from the draft by paying $300. Or, he could pay another man to go in his place. Rich men could afford to do that, but poor men could not.

When the first names were called for the draft in New York City, there were riots. For four days, 50,000 people ran through the streets, burning houses and robbing stores. The rioters blamed black people for the war. They burned down an orphanage that cared for black children. Hundreds of black people were killed or tortured. White people who had spoken out against slavery were attacked.

Events during the war showed black people the problems they would face after the war. The abolition of slavery was not enough. Black people still faced white prejudice which would not allow them full equality. For many years to come, lynch mobs and race riots were part of the black experience in the North and in the South.

[41]

6

War and

Women

In the North and South, all the politicians who ran the country and all the generals who ran the armies were white men. Women had no chance to make any of the big decisions about war or peace, but their lives were profoundly affected by the war. Their homes were burned; their sons and husbands were killed.

Neither in the North nor the South were women allowed to join the army. A few women did manage to find their way around this rule. There was Malinda Blalock of North Carolina. When her husband, Keith, was asked to join the army he said he would not go without his wife. The recruiter agreed and signed up Malinda under the name of Sam. The three kept the secret, and Malinda lived the life of a soldier until her husband was discharged for physical unfitness. Malinda then told the colonel her secret, and she was sent home with Keith.

Other women served their cause as spies. Washington was

on the border between the North and the South. The city was full of soldiers and politicans and badly kept military secrets. The men were lonely, and attractive women found ways of persuading them to tell their secrets. Some women went farther afield. Pauline Cushman was an actress who found it possible to travel in the South and bring information back to the North.

Nursing was one kind of work that men allowed women to do. Until the Civil War, the United States Army had no real organization to take care of the wounded. But now there were thousands and thousands of sick and wounded soldiers close to home. Newspaper reporters wrote stories about them. Many men were hurt in battles not far from Washington, the nation's capital, and not far from friends and relatives. Public opinion forced the army to do something. Dorothea Dix was well known for her reform work in prisons and hospitals. She was put in charge of finding and training nurses for the Union Army hospitals. Miss Dix was sixty. "A kind old soul, but queer" was one description of her. She thought that nurses should be over thirty, strong, and homely. Army doctors were not at all sure that they wanted nurses. Someone like Miss Dix was needed. She was strong, opinionated, and used to dealing with people who did not want to change.

Clara Barton, who was later to found the American Red Cross, first learned of the need for such an organization when she cared for the wounded on Civil War battlefields.

Women volunteered as nurses for many reasons. Some wanted to serve their country or the antislavery cause. Some came out of pity for the suffering men. Others came because for the first time in their lives they found the chance to work at something interesting and worthwhile. Louisa May Alcott

Women acted as spies for both sides. Pauline Cushman was an actress who collected information for the Union cause while appearing as an actress in the South. She was discovered and sentenced to be hanged. When Southern troops withdrew in Tennessee, she was left behind. Later, dressed in a Union uniform, she lectured about her adventures.

spoke for many women when she said: "Help needed, and I love nursing, and must let out my pent-up energy in some new way . . . I want new experiences, and am sure to get 'em if I go."

Whatever their reasons, all the nurses went into hard work and danger. Hospitals were not clean places. The causes of infection were not understood. Louisa May Alcott caught typhoid fever while she was nursing the wounded in Washington.

The Union government also formed the Sanitary Commission to help take care of the health needs of soldiers. The Commission tried to make both camps and hospitals healthier places. Camps were cleaned up and hospitals provided with medicines, bandages, and better food. The Commission ran convalescent homes in which wounded soldiers could recover and helped to bring the sick and injured and their families together again.

The Commission was headed by men, but much of the work was done by women. All over the country, women raised money by cake sales and carnivals to buy supplies for the Commission to distribute. For many women, this was their first experience with organized charitable work.

As men went off to join the army, women found more jobs open to them. Male teachers joined up, and women took their place in the classroom. There were more factory jobs open to women as the demand for uniforms and weapons for the army grew. It was during the Civil War that women began working in government offices in Washington in large numbers.

The South could not provide women with job opportunities like those in the North. Southern women nursed their wounded, and their difficulties were even greater than in the North because of the shortage of drugs and medical supplies.

☆ WOMEN AND POLITICS

Leaders of the women's movement had worked closely with the abolitionists before the war. They did not stop now.

When Lincoln was first elected, many people were afraid that he would not take a strong enough stand against slavery. (Just as many people were afraid that he would take too strong a stand.) Soon after he became president, Susan Anthony, Elizabeth Cady Stanton, and Lucretia Mott went on a tour of New York State. They used slogans like: "No Compromise With Slave Holders" and "Immediate and Unconditional Emancipation." This was too radical for most of the citizens of New York. When the women spoke in Syracuse, a mob of men rushed into the hall, threatening them with knives and pistols. In Albany, the mayor sympathized with them. He sat on the platform with a pistol ready to protect them.

All through the war, abolitionists tried to persuade Lincoln to move more quickly to free the slaves. In 1863 Charles Sumner of Massachusetts introduced into Congress a constitutional amendment to end slavery forever.

Susan Anthony and Elizabeth Stanton knew that here was a job for them. They knew that Congress would never pass that amendment unless members felt many people wanted it.

They called a meeting of women from all over the country saying: "Woman is equally interested and responsible with man in the settlement of this problem of self-government; therefore let us not stand idle spectators now."

The women met in New York. They decided to collect a million signatures of people who wanted the amendment— who wanted to see slavery end. The Women's National Loyal League was formed, with Elizabeth Stanton as president and

Elizabeth C. Stanton and Susan B. Anthony worked together in the women's movement for many years. Before the Civil War, they collected thousands of signatures on petitions asking for women to be given some rights. They worked with the Abolitionists to try to end slavery. During the war, they founded the National Women's Loyal League to fight for a quick end to slavery.

Susan Anthony as secretary. All over the country, women went out, asking their neighbors to sign the petition. They didn't collect a million signatures, but they did collect 400,000 signatures asking Congress to pass an amendment abolishing slavery. In August 1864 the petition was presented to Congress. The next year the Thirteenth Amendment was passed.

☆ WOMEN AT HOME

Some of the hardest work during the war was done by the women, in both the North and South. They kept the farms producing while the men were in the army. They and their children tried to do the work of men, planting and plowing and reaping. They tried to earn a little money selling eggs or quilts, doing sewing for other families. In the South, women were left to run the plantations, and they tried to change from cotton to food production. On the small hill farms, families struggled on, trying to raise enough to feed themselves.

In many parts of the country, in the Shenandoah Valley and along the coastal plains of Georgia, and in many other parts of the South, women saw the farms they had tried to save, burned and pillaged. All over the country, wives heard the news that their husbands would not be coming home.

During the long years of war, women learned new skills, a new self-reliance. More and more women learned each year that they could work as hard as men. More and more women felt that they deserved equality.

After the war, they learned that equality was not to be theirs. The Fourteenth Amendment that gave the vote to black men used the word "male" to make sure that everyone understood that women were still not allowed to vote.

[48]

7

Bullets and

Battles

☆ NAVAL WARFARE

Only by selling cotton to England and other European countries could the South buy war supplies. Lincoln decided to blockade the Confederacy. Northern ships sailed up and down the coast to keep Southern ships from going in or out of harbor. At the beginning of the war, Lincoln had only ninety ships to patrol thousands of miles of coastline. Blockade running (avoiding the patrol ships) became much like a popular sport. Daring Confederate sailors took their ships out to foreign ports and brought them back loaded with goods for the hungry South. Northern shipyards then went into full production. By the end of the war, the Union Navy had 670 ships.

Some of these ships were of a kind that had never sailed the seas before. When the war began, Union sailors scuttled and sank the ships they had to leave behind in the naval yard at Norfolk, Virginia. Confederates salvaged the *Merrimack*.

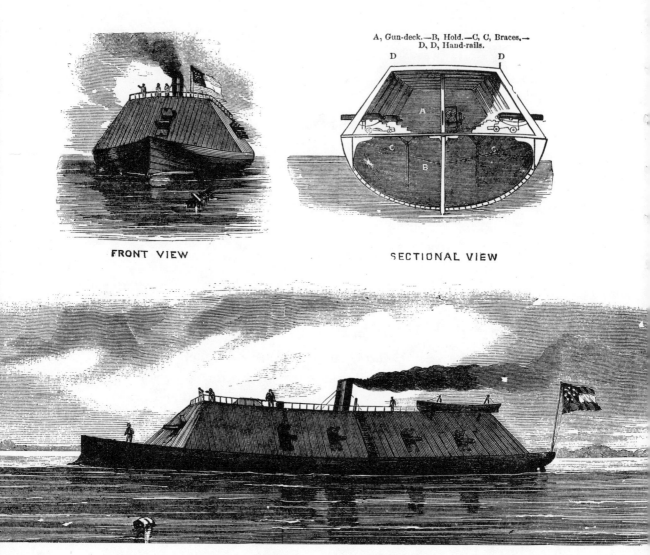

FRONT VIEW

A, Gun-deck.—B, Hold.—C, C, Braces.—
D, D, Hand-rails.

SECTIONAL VIEW

*The South was never able to build as many ironclad ships as the North.
People in the North and South were fascinated by the details of this new
kind of ship. This drawing was published in* Harpers Weekly, *one of the
magazines that people in the North read to keep up with the war news.*

They renamed her the *Virginia,* but the world continued to call her the *Merrimack.* Her masts and wooden superstructure were torn away and replaced with stout oak planks sheathed with iron plating. She looked like a floating fortress from which ten guns poked. Her iron prow could ram and sink any wooden ship afloat. The first victims were Union ships.

But the Northern shipyards built their own ironclad ship —the *Monitor.* People called the *Monitor* a "cheesebox on a raft," and that was what it looked like. The deck was flat with a round turret on top. The turret turned so that its guns could be pointed in any direction.

The *Merrimack* and the *Monitor* were two of the ugliest ships that ever floated. The battle they fought was one of the most decisive in history, even though it was a draw. The *Monitor* could not sink the *Merrimack.* The Confederate vessel was chased back to Norfolk and never came out again to bother Union ships. Northern shipyards went on to build many more ironclads, with which they controlled the seas and the western rivers. And the battle between the *Monitor* and the *Merrimack* also meant the end of wooden ships all over the world. From then on all navies wanted iron ships.

Lincoln thus was able to cut the South off from the outside world. She could not sell her cotton, or buy clothing, guns, ammunition, medicines—or any of those things she needed from other countries to survive.

☆ GENERAL ULYSSES S. GRANT

In those days of poor roads and few railroads, the Mississippi River was the greatest highway in the country. Steamboats and flatboats went up and down. People traveled on the river and so did the cotton and grain and furs and lumber that were bought and sold.

The war in the West was fought for control of the rivers, especially the Mississippi. The Union had two great assets in the West. One was the gunboats, the ironclads that destroyed the Confederate ships and the forts along the banks.

The other great asset was General Ulysses S. Grant. He had once before been a professional soldier, but when war broke out he was in the leather business and was not doing very well. Back he went into the army. Grant never looked like a professional soldier. Usually he wore a private's uniform, badly in need of cleaning. Most of the time he had a rather worn-looking cigar in his mouth. When a battle was at its hottest, he was often found sitting and whittling. An officer once suggested that General Grant should move because enemy gunfire was coming close. Grant said that it would make more sense to bring up more guns and drive the enemy back. He was impatient with people who worried about what might happen.

Grant first proved himself in the West. Using gunboats to attack from the water while his troops came overland, he captured Confederate forts along the Mississippi. At Shiloh, in Tennessee, he fought a desperate land battle. After that he went back to the river and besieged the city of Vicksburg, in Mississippi, for six weeks. The population was starved into submission. With Grant's victory at Vicksburg on July 4, 1863, the tide turned. Now the North had a great general. Now the Union controlled the Mississippi. The Confederacy was split in two. Louisiana, Arkansas, and Texas were cut off from the other Southern states.

General Ulysses S. Grant—
the man who finally won the
war for Lincoln. People often
criticized him because his
uniform and his personal
habits were sloppy. When
someone told Lincoln that
Grant drank too much, the
President said that if he
could find out what brand
Grant drank, he would send
bottles to his other generals.

General Jeb Stuart of the Confederate Army
was the most brilliant cavalry commander
on either side. He often rode all around
the Union Army so that he could keep General Lee informed of the enemy's exact
strength and movements. On one raid he
captured 1,200 horses. For the first years
of the war, the Confederate cavalry was
much better than the Union cavalry. The
Southern men—most of them from the
country—were better riders, and their
leaders were more imaginative.

☆ SLAUGHTER AT GETTYSBURG

That same week the South suffered another terrible defeat. Lee was ready to make his second attempt to invade the North. Ragged Southern troops, with few supplies left, marched northward to the town of Gettysburg, Pennsylvania. Soldiers, riding ahead in search of food, ran into Union cavalry. The battle that started by chance turned into the bloodiest of the Civil War. Neither side really knew what was happening or where. When the fighting began, neither side had many men on hand. All that first day more troops poured in. The Confederates managed to push the Yankees back.

By the second day of battle, the situation had changed. The North was now in possession of the high ground. Two days of heavy Southern losses followed as attempts were made to break Northern strongholds.

For the last Southern attack—Pickett's Charge—every Southern soldier available was used. But the men were charging uphill. At the top of the hill, Northern troops knelt behind stone fences. They fired down on the waves of men climbing uphill. Twelve thousand men fell in one hour. Those who did manage to reach Union lines fought hand to hand with Union troops. But the Southerners had no strength left. Northern reinforcements arrived and pushed the Confederates back to their own lines.

Horrified at the slaughter, Lee apologized to his troops and pulled together what remained of his army for the long retreat back to Virginia. A seventeen-mile-long wagon train carried the wounded.

Southern casualties numbered 28,000; 23,000 Northerners

fell. Fifty-one thousand American casualties in one three-day battle!

Never again were Southern troops to invade the North. From now on the war was fought in the fields and cities of the South.

☆ GRANT GOES SOUTH

In the spring of 1864, Lincoln appointed Grant, the man who had been so successful in the West, as General-in-Chief of the United States Army.

General Grant understood that taking Richmond was not his first aim. His job was to destroy Lee's army and the Southern countryside on which it depended for supplies. He sent General Phil Sheridan to burn the farms in the Shenandoah Valley. He sent General William Tecumseh Sherman marching through Georgia, setting fire to farms and barns and crops in the fields. Grant was making sure that the South could not feed its army or its people.

"I can make Georgia howl!" said Sherman. This kind of warfare made the whole Confederacy howl.

The blockade of her ports cut the South off from European goods. There were no factories in the South to make the guns or ammunition she needed. Her armies could not fight without them. There were no medicines for sick soldiers or civilians. Lee's army was in rags. Many of the soldiers had no shoes. Northern troops tore up railroad lines so that food could not be sent from one part of the South to another.

Sherman and Sheridan burned the farms. There was no food for soldiers or civilians. Southern cities were in flames.

[55]

Grant set out from Washington to destroy Lee's army. The Union and Confederate armies fought through the Virginia countryside, where they had fought for three years, but this fighting was different.

Grant was not afraid of Lee. He did not spend his time wondering what the enemy was going to do. He knew what he was doing—and he did not stop. Grant led his army on no matter how many men were killed. He knew that the Union Army could get more men. Whenever he needed them, there were more men and more guns. There were no more men and no more guns in the South for Lee. Time was running out for the South.

Thousands of Union and Confederate soldiers were killed as Grant pressed on. Lee used every maneuver possible to delay the army as it came closer and closer to Richmond.

The Federal army was much better organized than when the war began. These were veteran troops, well-armed and well-trained, not the green soldiers who panicked in that first battle at Bull Run.

But there was still a shortage of well-trained officers. No one ever did find out how to make sure that Grant's orders were obeyed. Nothing that Lee did helped the Confederacy as much as the mistakes of Grant's own officers. After weeks of costly fighting, Grant decided to head for Petersburg, not Richmond. Several railroad lines met at Petersburg. If Grant controlled them, he could cut Richmond off from the rest of the Confederacy. Petersburg was held by only a few troops. Grant sent William F. Smith off to capture the city. After capturing most of the fortifications around the city, Smith delayed,

*After a battle, bodies littered the fields where
battle had been fought. The photographers and
artists who followed the army made people all
over the country aware of the terrible killing.*

waiting for reinforcements. That gave Lee time to move his army to Petersburg. By the time Grant arrived, the city was well defended. He had to settle down for a nine-month siege before Confederate troops gave up the city.

The siege could have ended long before that, if there had not been more blunders. A group of soldiers who had been coal miners in Pennsylvania decided that they knew how to get into Petersburg. They dug a long tunnel, so long that anyone, Union or Confederate, who heard rumors about the tunnel did not believe them. At the end of the tunnel, the miners placed a charge of explosive. When it was fired, a great hole appeared in the defenses of Petersburg. The whole Union Army could have walked through. But there was another mix-up. A division of black soldiers had been specially trained to lead the attack, but some people objected to black soldiers being in such an important position. At the last minute, they were replaced by white soldiers who were already worn and weary from fighting. Added to that problem, two of the division commanders who were supposed to lead the attack lay asleep, dead drunk. Again, the Confederates had time on their side. They closed up the hole.

While Grant sat outside Petersburg, the war went on. Sherman and Sheridan continued to destroy the Confederate countryside. Life at home went on, too. People were tired of the war. Many white Northerners felt that they did not want to fight for black freedom. Abraham Lincoln was elected president again in 1864 but with a small majority of 400,000 votes out of 4,000,000. Even Lincoln had not been sure that he would be elected again.

8

The End of the War

March 4, 1865, was a rainy day. Women who came in crinolines to see Mr. Lincoln sworn in as president for the second time, found their wide skirts splashed with mud. But in spite of the weather, Washington was a happy city. The war was coming to a close. Cheers rang out when Lincoln rose to speak. Four years before he had spoken of the coming war. Now he spoke of the coming peace. He knew that bitter quarrels were going on in Washington and the rest of the country about the kind of peace the nation needed. There were men who wanted to punish the South, to make its people suffer more.

Lincoln disagreed. He felt that once the two warring sections became one nation again they must learn to live together in trust. They must learn to help each other and to forgive each other. Lincoln spoke to all the people:

"With malice toward none; with charity for all . . . let us

strive on to finish the work we are in; to bind up the nation's wounds; to care for him who shall have borne the battle, and for his widow, and his orphan. . . ."

Lincoln and the Washington crowds were right. The war was almost over.

The next month, Petersburg fell. President Jefferson Davis and his cabinet fled from Richmond. For a few days, Lee tried to hold on. He and his army raced across the Virginia fields, pursued by the Union Army. Lee's troops had no food. They were in rags. More fighting would only mean more killing. The Confederacy no longer had hope, and Lee surrendered to Grant at Appomattox Courthouse in Virginia.

The two generals sat down in a farmhouse there and agreed to terms. They looked as they had always looked. Lee was the Virginia gentleman in a fine uniform. Grant wore a dirty private's uniform.

Grant understood Lincoln's feeling about making a peace that would help the whole country recover. He allowed the men and officers of Lee's army to take their horses home with them so that they could start the spring plowing. When the men of the Union Army began to fire their guns to celebrate the victory, Grant ordered them to stop. He explained: ". . . we did not want to exult over their downfall."

But the dreams of Lincoln and Grant were not to be.

On April 14, 1865, just a few days after the meeting at Appomattox, Lincoln went to the theater in Washington. Mrs. Lincoln persuaded him to go because she felt that he needed to relax.

As the president sat watching the play, he was shot. The

assassin was John Wilkes Booth, an actor, and one of a small band of conspirators who were quickly captured.

The country was horrified. Everyone had hoped that the hatred and killing were over. Lincoln's body was taken by train back to Illinois. All along the way people wept as they watched the black draped train pass by. They felt that the country had lost the one man who could lead them back to peace and a full rich life.

The war was over. But the problems that had caused the war had not been solved.

The North was stronger and richer than ever before. Factory owners had made money selling guns and clothes and tents and wagons to the army. Farmers made money selling food to the army. Thousands of new immigrants arrived from Europe. New railroads united California and the East.

The South, however, was much poorer than before the war. Her factories and crops were burned. Railroad lines were torn up. Cities were destroyed.

The South needed help to rebuild her cities, her farms, her railroads. With Lincoln dead, Congress and the new president, Andrew Johnson, quarreled bitterly about how to treat the South. In the end, no one helped the people of the Confederacy rebuild their lives. Bitterness lingered in the ruins. Northerners went South. Some went with the army. Some went to help, building schools and bringing medical services. Others went South to make money from the misery of the South. These men were sometimes called "carpetbaggers" because they often carried their possessions in bags made from carpet.

In the North and South, women found that their position

had not changed. They were still not allowed to vote. There were no new careers for them. Women who had kept the farms producing found that the farms still belonged to their husbands. Louisa May Alcott went home to Cambridge. She went back to writing stories to support her father and mother and three sisters. When she wrote her most famous book, *Little Women,* she pretended that it was her father who had gone to war. (In the end, like all her sisters, she died of tuberculosis.)

Black people in the North and South found that freedom was not enough. Those who had been slaves were free, but free without education or land or money. Most had no way to earn a living for themselves and their children. White people in the North and South were not prepared to accept blacks as equals. Black families had to live in the worst houses and send their children to the worst schools. Most black men could not get jobs. Most black women could only find work cleaning the houses and taking care of the children of white women. Blacks who tried to change things were threatened. They were jailed and sometimes killed.

The United States was one country again, but still not a country ready to accept equality for all its people.

Glossary

ABOLITIONISTS: people who wanted to end slavery

BLOCKADE: stopping things or people from going into or out of a place

CAVALRY: soldiers who ride horses into battle

CONFEDERACY: the Southern states that left the United States to form the Confederate States of America

DEMOCRATIC PARTY: the oldest political party in the United States. During the Civil War it split North and South.

THE EMANCIPATION PROCLAMATION: issued by Abraham Lincoln, it said that "Persons held as slaves" in areas "in rebellion against the United States" would be free on and after January 1, 1863.

FIELD HAND: a slave who worked on the farm and not in the master's house

FOUNDRY: a place where metal is melted and molded

HAVERSACK: a bag used by soldiers to carry food

MISSOURI COMPROMISE: when Missouri was admitted as a state in 1820, Congress agreed that there should be no slavery in the Louisiana Purchase north of the latitude 36° 30′

PLANTATION: a large farm in the South. Most of the work on the plantation was done by slaves

RECRUIT: a man who joined the army voluntarily

REPUBLICAN PARTY: formed in the 1850s to fight against the extension of slavery and for higher tariffs. It first ran a candidate for president in 1856 and elected Lincoln in 1860.

SNIPER: a person shooting from a hiding place

UNION: the Northern states during the Civil War

WAGON TRAIN: many wagons traveling together

Books to Read

The First Book of Civil War Land Battles. Trevor Nevitt Dupuy. Franklin Watts.

The First Book of Civil War Naval Action. Trevor Nevitt Dupuy. Franklin Watts.

Lincoln and the Emancipation Proclamation. Frank B. Latham. Franklin Watts.

Thunder at Gettysburg. Patricia Lee Gauch. Coward McCann.

Across Five Aprils. Irene Hunt. Follett.

Corrie and the Yankee. Mimi Cooper Levy. Viking.

Harriet Beecher Stowe. Noel Gerson. Praeger.

Gettysburg: Tad Lincoln's Story. F. N. Monjo. Windmill/ Dutton.

Lincoln and the Emancipation Proclamation. Frank B. Latham. Franklin Watts.

Civil War Naval Actions. Trevor Nevitt Dupuy. Franklin Watts.

Civil War Land Battles. Trevor Nevitt Dupuy. Franklin Watts.

Index